EL JARDÍN DE LAS ROSAS SILVESTRES

ExLibric

MIKAEL RIBBING GREN

EL JARDÍN DE LAS ROSAS SILVESTRES

EXLIBRIC

ANTEQUERA 2025

EL JARDÍN DE LAS ROSAS SILVESTRES
© Mikael Ribbing Gren
Diseño de portada: Dpto. de Diseño Gráfico Exlibric

Iª edición

© ExLibric, 2025.

Editado por: ExLibric
c/ Cueva de Viera, 2, Local 3
Centro Negocios CADI
29200 Antequera (Málaga)
Teléfono: 952 70 60 04
Fax: 952 84 55 03
Correo electrónico: exlibric@exlibric.com
Internet: www.exlibric.com

ISBN: 979-13-87944-58-2
Depósito Legal: MA 1444-2025

Impresión: PODiPrint
Impreso en Andalucía – España

Nota de la editorial: ExLibric pertenece a Innovación y Cualificación S. L.

MIKAEL RIBBING GREN

EL JARDÍN DE LAS ROSAS SILVESTRES

Índice

LOS MUSEOS

Gaviotas dispersas
sobre ruinas persas,
cadáveres de elefantes
sobre pirámides con diamantes,
carnívoras como panteras
sobre los restos de las dinastías severas.
Gritos lejanos
sobre mitos profanos
llenan de tristeza los llanos.
La hierba verde crece
donde el espacio se lo ofrece,
llorones,
gatos por montones.
Restos de huesos
soportan el peso,
sesos blancos y grises,
el viento con sus caricias
despeja los restos.
Cóndores si hubiera
se ríen y se jactan
del hallazgo que impacta a
los sentidos de los peregrinos,
que caminan con trapos de lino

por bosques de pinos,
hasta llegar al altar de los caídos,
huesos fríos
rodeados de gatitos críos.
Los recogen en balsas
y se los llevan adonde sepa Dios,
al Occidente prepotente,
que los guarda en museos
como reliquias,
como trofeos,
para que los vean,
para que las multitudes lean
y para que miren
en libros viejos
los restos de los festejos.

LA FILOSOFÍA DE LA PASIFLORA

Tal vez por alguna razón,
en un telescopio no se ven las cosas como son,
quizás solo desde la mente
se nota la perfección
de un número,
de un sistema solar,
visto en una pasiflora.
Durante el Renacimiento
pusieron el acento
en un evento «real»,
pero ¿y si no era tal?
Vieron en lo grande la imperfección,
mientras que los antiguos creyentes,
entristecidos con botellas de ron,
se acordaron de esos días,
de esas creencias del corazón,
que brotaron de la lógica y de la aritmética
bajo la pura razón,
en armonía con la estética.
Pero la medición frenética
y la observación
terminaron con una era
y dejó a los antiguos creyentes
caídos entre botellas de ron.

LOS PENSAMIENTOS

Una ardilla anda por las ramas,
mientras que el águila persigue a su presa desde lejos;
un cerebro en llamas,
viendo desde la caverna solamente reflejos;
la verdad son los rayos del sol,
y la mentira, las siluetas y sombras,
la verdad negra como carbón;
la intuición, rayos en forma de ondas
que vienen desde la nada
a la mente de un organismo,
vestido en trapos o de seda,
y entra al profundo abismo
de la conciencia.
Al medium, tal vez,
al mundo físico,
invisible o camuflado
como entre las rocas un pez.
Tal vez fea a veces,
o bella de colores brillantes,
una misma especie, pero variados los peces,
mirando hacia el futuro o al pasado.
No creas que uno es mejor que los otros,
pues son muy diferentes,

similares a nosotros,
a veces brillantes,
pero a menudo oscuras las mentes.
Me hago la pregunta
sobre un tal más allá;
será militar, así como una junta,
quizás en el futuro se sabrá.
Anguilas por montones,
águilas en los montes,
unos cuantos borrachos llorones,
un gato espiando horizontes.
El esplendor y la riqueza
se mezclan con lo incierto y lo mezquino,
envenenadas o no las copas de vino sobre la mesa,
probar o no esas copas de vino,
arriesgarse y suplicar al olimpo
por suerte, quizás,
a los dioses del oro y del vino tinto,
o caer al abismo depende de lo que me das.

NOSTALGIA

Pelo negro como el carbón,
me miraste desde atrás en el taxi,
hace tantos años ya.
Caminamos juntos en la playa,
cantaste en el autobús,
al fin del mundo.
Tocaste algo muy profundo,
pero lo negaste todo,
de tu modo,
y quizás sea mejor así.
La ciudad se llenaba de niebla,
el gato comía pollo,
y yo me pasaba rollos.
Vivíamos en una cabaña,
y me escribiste sobre una araña
que me dio miedo.
Caminamos por la calle,
recuerdo cada detalle:
tu abrigo azul largo,
tocándome suavemente,
tal vez sin querer;
tu aura me atraía,
hasta el punto que creía

que eras mía.
Pero a pesar de los paisajes,
los músicos
y los bosques jurásicos,
al final desapareciste para siempre.
Estaba todo en mi mente,
así fue mi juventud.
Después, tal vez vivo más,
pero siento menos.
Recuerdo tu mirada melancólica
contemplando el mar,
y como un viejo borracho
esta mañana la nostalgia me hace llorar.

LA ISLA

Tomo mate
encima de un yate,
mientras mi corazón late.
Suena el motor,
como los truenos de Thor;
es una máquina fabulosa,
una cosa tan hermosa,
muy caro y extremadamente raro,
en lo lejano veo la luz de un faro.
Encima la luna brilla todavía,
toda amarilla;
sé que hay tiburones aquí
pero no me amenazan a mí.
Voy a una isla desierta,
mi imaginación despierta.
Aquí, sobre las olas del mar,
me siento como un zar
de la antigua Rusia,
lejos de las calles sucias,
lejos de la gente,
dejo que los pensamientos bailen en mi mente
sobre lo que tengo enfrente.
En unos días llegaremos,

sonarán los frenos
y, en la playa,
con las barrigas llenas de vino,
nos reiremos sobre arena fina.
El océano me da mareos,
a la vez que aumenta mis deseos
de respirar el aire de un mundo sereno.

Solo sé que nada sé

Quién es el dueño de mis sueños.
Quién dirige mis pensamientos.
Quién me regala pasiones.
Quién soy yo, sino una sombra
que se mueve sin saber por qué,
que no sabe, que no tiene fe.
Quién dirige mi mano
al tomar una taza de té o de café.
¿Está todo resuelto
o todavía en misterio envuelto?
Entendemos muy poco del universo
en el que estamos inmersos,
muy poco del cerebro y del alma.
Lo importante es mantener la calma,
proceder como si nada,
caminar según principios más o menos rígidos,
nadar en un río de pensamientos líquidos,
estar en el presente
y ver lo que tengo enfrente,
apaciguar mi mente,
caminar entre la gente
sin volverse loco

al preguntarse por qué,
rayándose el coco
por lo que no sé.

EL ESCAPE

Peces de colores brillantes
brillan como diamantes
bajo el sol que penetra
la superficie con sus rayos.
Muchos se sumergen
en la cueva bajo el mar,
y se dejan llevar
por las corrientes submarinas,
algas verdes claras
se mueven.
Encima llueve,
y un arcoíris aparece, hermoso, sobre el agua;
bajo el mar todo es calma;
Allí, en mi imaginación,
descansa el alma.
Bajo una palmera con una botella de ron
y las llamas de una hoguera,
estoy sin camiseta,
bajo una llovizna cristalina
sobre arena fina.
Más allá, una aleta
de un tiburón se acerca,
el graznido de un cuervo entre los árboles.

Un loro guarda mi tesoro de oro
en la cueva bajo la isla,
olvidado por los moros
en antiguos tiempos.
Los rayos del sol
entran y alumbran las monedas
mientras los peces coloridos suben a la superficie.
Trepo una palmera para sacar un coco,
el loro grita como loco,
está preocupado,
porque siempre estoy a su lado,
y él al mío,
como los peces amarillos,
como los grillos que, juntos,
cantan con chirridos su canción
al tomarme echado el ron.
Debajo del arcoíris, decían
los marineros mientras sonreían,
se esconde el tesoro de los moros
guardado por un loro,
y yo con mi locura
lo fui a buscar.
Amar el oro,
el coro
de los grillos,
los peces amarillos.

Aquí me quedo sedado,
con mi pájaro verde al lado,
mareado;
al fin y al cabo,
deseo el ambiente tropical,
lejos de todo el mal,
de la capital.
Lejos de Barcelona
y la gente con sus intereses.
¿Es todo lo que ofreces?
El calor se impone durante meses,
y la lluvia se ausenta;
hay que pagar la renta,
el tiempo fluye como agua lenta
y busco en mi mente un escape.
Todavía mi corazón late,
a pesar de los yates,
los coches caros,
los aros de la vanidad,
y las manos de la caridad.
La gente humilde tirada en la calle,
bajo trapos y cartones,
desearía algo semejante, un valle,
donde escapar del sistema,
de los problemas,
de las hienas

que te quieren comer
y romper tus huesos.
Somos todos presos,
como momias envueltas en yeso.

EL INSPECTOR DISPERSO

«¿Dónde están los gossos[1]?»,
se preguntan aturdidos los Mossos
d'Esquadra[2],
mientras se reúnen en una cuadra
del viejo Eixample.
—¡Aquí estoy! —ladra una perra dama,
mientras muerde una pastanaga[3] en Praga.
El inspector nada escucha,
lucha,
se mira el ombligo,
pero la maduixa[4] se ha perdido en la ducha,
¡Pucha!
¡Qué chucha!
Tal vez en una frutería encontrarás tu tesoro,
quizás vendido por un moro
o por un chino vestido de lino.
Un viejo del barrio se pregunta
por el civismo catalán.

---

[1] En catalán, «gossos» significa «perros».
[2] Los Mossos d'Esquadra (Mozos de Escuadra) son la policía autonómica de Cataluña.
[3] En castellano, «zanahoria».
[4] En castellano, «fresa».

Pero no es el afán,
del perro galán,
que se compara con los hermosos,
mientras traga un trozo de pan.
Las gaviotas se ríen desde los techos,
comen los restos,
y los pobres mossos se llenan de pretextos.
Se mueven de cuadra en cuadra
y escuchan un perro que ladra.
«¡Independentismo!», se escucha desde Besalú,
mientras todo lo mira Jesús sobre la cruz.
Por la noche llegaste
y cruzaste la avenida Diagonal,
pero los pobres mossos miraban mal;
no lo vieron cruzar,
estaban ya al lado del mar,
en Barceloneta,
lo cual fue la meta
del pobre inspector disperso,
que ya no cantaba,
se tragaba
maduixes por montones,
sobre las ruinas del Raval
donde se esconde el mal,
y le robaron el móvil
y, además, cogió covid-19

que los chinos trajeron,
como el arroz tres delicias que vendieron
en sus bares,
que están por todos los lugares.

VIAJE ASTRAL

Debajo del mar,
en la era de las lemurias,
yacen los peces feos y grises,
con sus miradas tristes.
Las muñecas de tela muertas en la arena,
yo los veo desde mi cabina del futuro,
como un arqueólogo
mirando el pasado en las estrellas,
viendo pasar las huellas
y las vidas cotidianas
de épocas pasadas,
hasta llegar a la superficie,
jugando en el agua con delfines arcaicos,
¿Por qué están tristes los peces feos?

EN CHILE

Prostitutas, mendigos,
evangélicos y perdidos,
perros rastreros,
duros marineros.
País de la almeja
y del puma,
país que refleja
sombras de espuma.
Negocios que cantan,
borrachos que pelean,
desesperado el llanto
del mar que murmura.
País de la fruta
y del vino,
tomando la ruta
respirando aire frío,
en el coche que nos lleva a la playa,
lejos del ruido y la sierra.
Fuera de la casa donde vivo
y de las plumas que caen de la perra,
dominados en las filas
de una burocracia cruel.
Calvo el desierto
por la lluvia infiel.

EL PAÍS DE LAS TUMBAS

Endeudar, desnudar a Neruda
en el momento de su candidatura,
suenan los tambores y se caen las flores tristes,
que cantan su bravura.
Los chilenos se van a la funa[5],
gritan en su funeral,
aullando hacia la luna,
cerca de su mural,
donde suenan las metralletas
y caen las bombas.
El país de las tumbas,
de la grandiosa bandera
que echa sus colores a un cielo azul.
En la plaza de Armas
gritan las palmeras
en el viento cruel,
del aliento del pasar y del pasado,
cuerpos arrastrados, atropellados, lanzados
por el río Mapocho[6].

---

[5] En Chile, «funa» se refiere a un acto público de denuncia o agravio
contra una persona o entidad, generalmente frente a su domicilio o sede,
para dar a conocer una situación reprochable o alertar a otros sobre ella.
[6] El río Mapocho es el agua proveniente de los Andes que fluye por

Cuarenta grados,
el agua enfermante,
el anhelo del agua refrescante
de la corriente de Humboldt,
que atraviesa sus costas, sus orillas frías,
en medio del verano.
Cantan los poetas y los delincuentes,
los senadores
en sus sillas de cuero rojo escarlata.

---

la Región Metropolitana de Santiago y el principal de la capital llamada
Santiago de Chile.

EL NIDO DE LAS ÁGUILAS

De nuevo en el nido de las águilas, mirando tristes los trozos de algodón fríos pasando por fuera de las ventanas, fuera del balcón cubriendo la vista y las ganas de salir. Triste la ciudad y las ramas rotas de los árboles gigantescos que parecen gigantes hechos piedra, siluetas de constancia y cemento, un esqueleto que perdura, un esqueleto que se viste, endurecido por los años y por el tiempo, por los vientos, la lluvia, las tormentas y la nieve blanca.

EL BOSQUE

Me gustaría vivir en el bosque, caminar por las colinas, mirar el sol al reflejarse en los lagos, sentir el olor de los árboles, la humedad del aire al atardecer y los pájaros, para llenarme con naturaleza, la ropa con barro y lluvia; comer pescado fresco asado sobre el fuego, para sentirme humano, limpio como el cielo, un trozo de conciencia en la jaula coloreada que forma la sutil prisión con sus paredes de humo y transparencia, sus tapices verdes y las frías pinturas llenas de estrellas.

EL SEÑOR Y EL CUERVO

Una impasible franqueza
iluminaba el rostro del señor,
un aterido sentado en el tejado,
silencioso clamor
con el cuervo a su lado.
Impasible entre lluvia y sol
sobre su barraca hecha de chapa,
jugando entre las ráfagas el rol
de un simple punto en un mapa.

LOS CHILENISMOS

Caramba, por comer porotos me llaman roto,
por no tener ni cobre para alimentar al pobre,
por comer garbanzos me llaman Pancho,
siendo un Quijote me rechazan los chilotes.
Viejas cochinas se creen minas[7],
el folklore se muere, mi alma duele;
cuando el gallo no canta,
me desmayo;
cuando voy a la playa,
me echan la talla[8],
por no estar quemao me llaman quebrao[9].
La DINA[10] no rima porque carecen de tacto.
La Nueva Mayoría[11], pues, es un pacto,

---

[7] En Chile se usa la palabra «mina» para referirse a una mujer que es bonita o hermosa.

[8] En Chile se dice «echar la talla» al querer molestar a alguien diciendo que es un chiste o una broma.

[9] En Chile, la palabra «quebrado/a» se puede usar para describir a alguien que no está en control de sus emociones o acciones, o que tiene problemas de algún tipo.

[10] La Dirección de Inteligencia Nacional (DINA) fue la policía secreta de la dictadura militar de Augusto Pinochet en Chile entre los años 1973 y 1977.

[11] La Nueva Mayoría fue una coalición política chilena que juntaba a un conjunto de partidos de centroizquierda e izquierda, creada en 2013.

la política más rígida
que un inglés en Valparaíso.
Me dan risa las locuras de la misa,
y el olor a comedia trágica en la brisa.

DESDE BARCELONA

Las cotorras argentinas verdes
cantan en el parque frondoso de la Ciutadella;
burgueses disfrutan del ocio en el Hotel Vela;
libros de Neruda tirados en la calle
versan sobre una estrella;
los gatitos y pescadores
se tumban en los muelles.
Yo aquí, inventando poemas
de mi corazón llenos
y de mi inconsciente plenos,
como una fuente que chorrea
bellas doncellas sobre la arena.
Aquí hay que cuidarse el bolsillo,
porque hay robos;
yo sueño con mi castillo
cerca de un río.
Una entrada con una alfombra roja de seda,
allí mi imaginación se enreda
en las escaleras de mi castillo,
en eso me fío.
Una lámpara de cristal en el techo colgada
y unas escaleras de mármol en la majestuosa sala,
con torres, pasillos y murallas,

diversas habitaciones y valiosas piezas,
de eso rezas,
alma mía.
¿O no poseemos alma?
Esa reflexión igual me calma,
porque la materia también es espíritu,
como las vías del tren
soportan los trenes,
así viajamos sobre lo invisible,
como volando.
Me han dicho que la vida es un viaje,
entonces llevo mi equipaje
y subo a esas vías
con mi traje,
y camino como materia sobre el espíritu,
como un vagabundo rumbo
a San Petersburgo.
Mientras mis ansias de fumar
me destrozan los pulmones,
y gaviotas por montones
se ríen desde los techos de Barcelona;
que me seden,
que me dejen en coma.

EL CANTO DEL FLAMENCO SOLITARIO

Soy un flamenco, frágil y vulnerable,
vivo en el desierto de la sal.
Sueño con un río, un manantial,
un día como hoy paseo por las dunas de sal
y mis plumas rosadas
se desvanecen por la noche.
Cuando el cielo se llena de estrellas,
extraño mucho mi juventud
en las playas de Marbella.
Solo tengo una pierna,
pero soy muy tierna.
A veces voy al observatorio
para contemplar galaxias distantes,
o para esconderme de posibles carnívoros.

¡ÁNIMO!

Les deseo a todos suerte en este día
cuando llega la primavera,
el día también del trabajador,
cuando llega la luz de veras.
Desde las ruinas oscuras,
el clamor de los despojados,
que ven pisado su amor.
Que brille el copihue[12] rojo una mañana soleada
al son de instrumentos cristalinos,
bajo el cielo duro plateado,
tus rayos como relámpagos divinos.
Gotas de agua subiéndose al cielo en espirales,
cayendo después como flores de jazmín
en una taza blanca de té,
como estrellas fugaces
que se desvanecen en el mar del olvido.

---

[12] Es la flor nacional de Chile, muy linda y grande.

MELODÍAS DEL CIELO

Hace tiempo que no llora el cielo tanto,
no para su incansable lamento
sobre los llanos, prados y sobre el asfalto.
El olor a calle, hojas mojadas,
árboles brillando como caramelos,
en la oscuridad muy suavemente,
el cielo peina su cabello dulcemente.
Escucho el sonido de la televisión
que me llena de información,
sobre la antigua monarquía
que nos aleja de una soñada anarquía.
Salen de la tierra como gusanos cuando llueve,
el príncipe habla de altos ideales,
pero sus palabras caen más leves
que las cosquillas de las gotas
que hacen que las flores broten.
Tanto tiempo sin escuchar el cielo
con su melodía vacía,
el ritmo de la naturaleza
suena dentro de mi cabeza.
Fuera, del sonido no hay ni rastro,
como en la esfera celeste,
donde orbitan en la oscuridad los astros.

LA HISTORIA DE LOS TACONES

El hedor de tiempos pasados,
calles con excremento por todos lados,
sangre llena las manos
de los soldados que vuelven a su tierra.
No soportarías
las casas frías,
los trapos sucios
ni los ratones callejeros.
Así que inventaron los tacones,
para no pisar la mierda,
no para su belleza, bella dama,
ni para que se queje usted, don Dalai Lama,
ni tampoco para usarlos en la cama.
No, si hubieras caminado por los salones de Versalles
habrías tenido que taparte la nariz.
Como animales dejaban su orina
en los pasillos las bellas damas,
los nobles también llevaban tacones
y pañuelos perfumados envueltos en nubes,
dejando su fragancia por todos lados.
Veinte capas de maquillaje
entre esgrimas y mis rimas.
Una vez al año, antes de las bodas,

bañaban sus cuerpos sucios
por miedo al agua
que podía entrar
desde el mar
a sus entrañas.
Ciencias equivocadas,
revoluciones frustradas,
eso decoraba las costas del bello Mediterráneo.
Animales acuáticos en los mapas,
al fin del mundo
bajo el océano profundo,
alzaron sus banderas al navegar
al otro lado del mar,
para descubrir la tierra redonda,
pero, en vez de eso, las anacondas.
Y se murieron por falta de vitaminas
los marineros,
y hasta el clero,
que los acompañaban en sus aventuras,
escribían diarios,
que acabaron en tiendas de antigüedades,
sobre las atrocidades
de la leyenda negra.
Los indígenas se defendían con piedras,
mientras que los españoles usaban cañones y otras armas.
De repente sonaron las alarmas

desde los picos de las montañas,
pero era demasiado tarde.
Ya en fuego sus pueblos arden,
su honestidad sofocada por la astucia y la tecnología
de los intrusos de ultramar.
Ahora los llaman latinos
y viajan en autocar,
y vienen de visita,
pero tienen que trabajar
setenta horas a la semana,
y lo hacen sin quejas.
El centinela, el vigía,
no condena ni vigila.
La ley se demora
o por completo se ignora.

ROSAS EN LLAMAS

Velas que encienden rosas hermosas,
rojas sus hojas,
encima vuelan mariposas
entre la ceniza,
Buda y su sonrisa,
todo sin prisa,
todo con calma
para perfeccionar el alma.
Una brisa suena
y provoca un pequeño torbellino
sobre rosas rojas en fuego,
las hojas se ponen grises y negras
para subir con el viento luego.
La luna mira al niño en la cuna,
con su brillo amarillo,
un círculo con trozos de hielo,
un río que calma un anhelo frustrado,
las panteras negras y azules que nadan,
pedalean con sus patas.
Desde lo lejano suena una orquesta de latas
y las mariposas se desmayan,
y se queman en las velas,
el fuego lo devora todo,

el lodo se pone duro,
el muro de hielo se derrite,
El Buda enciende un puro en el fuego
y luego permite
que salgan las panteras mojadas,
rascándose las orejas que están llenas de almejas.
No hay ni rastro de quejas,
solo el brillo del fuego
y los restos de lo que devora,
la demora es la paciencia,
la divina ciencia.
La pasiflora y su prudencia
hacen que todo se duerma,
que nada se enferma,
panteras echadas en la hierba.
Así termina la historia,
sin euforia.

THE COSMOS

Clear moonrays fall
and reflect on a still surface
of shimmering pools
in a world without rules.
Soft darkness in a world of elves,
diving in wells of blue and white,
surrounded by black stone.
Silvery moon pearls shine
as I make a robe of a cloud
—soft as silk,
white as milk—
and it pushes me away
into a lush forest.
Humid scent and mushroom beds,
among trees —not palms—
oh, how it calms!
I jump into the Milky Way
and stay a while upon a star,
watching the dark winds.
The sphere spins
and I dive into the wind,
where I lose my soul in air so dark.
A spark of light from the sun

and clarity I won,
eaten by a silvery cosmic fish.
Soft tissue and tender flesh,
I stand up on my feet.
Within the bowel
as rainbows run to meet
the teeth of the silvery beast,
like a rope of colors.
In its winding moves I follow,
the beast dissolves and all is hollow,
an emptiness so fresh.
This is where I stay
if for time itself, I may,
wander astray,
on a dark empty bridge
to nowhere.

IN THE WATER

A man walks out on sunny water in the evening, cold air and the smell of lake and green trees. An engine made out of fish, filled with oil while the plants of the sea try to catch them, but they are evaded, or they are suffering the pressure of teeth. Down below the blue surface, lies an old shipwreck filled with narcotics and dead seamen whom the plants have eaten in half.

Suddenly, a rubber boat floats up with strings of bubbles and turns to the atmosphere for advice about their precarious situation, where is the state when I need it? I am filled with air, but I cannot scream, why am I not in the water? Why is the rainbow so fleeting? Am I perhaps dreaming?

And soon the moon fell like an arrow and pierced my yellow skin, it was then transformed into a moonboat filled with fishermen on the Pacific Ocean, where they drifted laughing at themselves and their moonshine dinner wine. Thee flying crystal glasses over the head of a whale and their splendidly isolated fingers dripping with thick silvery blood, for the waves to carry ashore, for the lazy fish to get stuck and travel abroad, without moving, while shimmering like never before.

WHITE PASSION DEMON PLAY

A blue fire, white passion demon play. Why did the stars circle around my head like loaded energy-filled atom particles? A critique of white reason, dissertation in the enactment of the white demons of North Africa. How did they come to be considered white and why wouldn't they develop beard-based cultural traits? There's a sugar pattern in my cup; it moves like a worm in the mud. A cannon of apples would make the day. Red, green, blue, apple flames, apple light… My computer is in stalemate; it has ceased to play. Its structural passions are sleeping, electric stars, demon array, rainbow dance in sunlight. I pray for rain. Why doesn't it rain? Shouldn't it snow? What are these colors in my mind? Products of a particle dance or an evil demon inviting consciousness for a dance in the peripheries. Ferries of truth, where is your wand, little child? Did you bring it from metaphysical domains, or do you carry it with you always? My beard is falling off, where is the rainduskhat when you need it? When you need to fill in the empty spaces… crack a nut in shining atmospheres, raining hamburgers, raining disgust. We are our galaxy; we were brought here by white dwarves. Everyone is drinking milk.

THE LAND OF THOUGHTS

The river runs quickly down the mountain; foam is jumping around like molecules in an electric chair. Plants with leaves like springs, as water comes, they bow and as water leaves, they shiver. A stone in the stream stands solid and stubborn, cleaving the flow for a moment.

Then there is the valley with the red fields of flowers that burst out like fountains in the wind. Small fires surround the calm flow of the river from the mountain. She left the blue ice to sleep in fields of passion, where wine is stirred with spices and boiled on the riverside.

Armies of bleak monsters with long fatless legs and arms are moving around outside the field. Corruption rages among them, yet they cannot enter the red landscape. They are dead, long dead, and the path to the flowery field has been forever shut. This is the land of thoughts and not the land of the real; no one must enter, and no one shall heal.

THE MAN, THE BIRD AND THE THEATRE OF THE ABSURD

Bird, I know you're disturbed by the rain that keeps falling.

I hear your complaints.

I will not comment on the matter of rain even if you ask me to, so you might as well shut that beak of yours.

Do not pressure me further; I have problems too… Yes, life in a community isn't what you think. You, egoist. You don't have history. You live in the present.

Bird, please be quiet and let me do my things. I am quite busy dancing in the theatre of the absurd.

Am I responsible for the rain? Be happy about what you have. Electrical cables to dwell on and great oaks in which to breed. You have all the spare time in the world; you don't have Fordism. Neither do you struggle with so much division of labor. Your world is not pictured on a map. You may fear the great birds of prey, but what other concerns do you have? Why don't you twitter for the old? Stop bothering me, I've had it with your lousy song.

A BEAUTIFUL NIGHTMARE

Dark rain on sparkling asphalt. The shimmering light of a lone lamp. The crawling beast is wreaking havoc in the ruins with the wooden cross. His limbs are shadows in the night, and his scream is that of the evil. An isolated black lake filled with women bathing in burning oil. Fried like potatoes in the heat while on the shores a pack of wolves gather showing their shining teeth. A dragon in the sky thunders and warm mist lays its hands upon nature.

THE HERON GOD

The sound of coffee being made, the rain that fell and these heavy green leaf-covered trees that never move. If we glide out for a moment over the calm river that hides behind the curtain of leaves, we will, after having passed the fountain by, reach a place where the master is the heron that lives there with his long sharp beak. He is present in the middle of the day when the air is heavy and humid. He is there when night comes, when the solemn streetlights cast their light on spider webs. I stand here watching the eyes of the heron flash and shine, that bird who lingers where water pours down a rocky slope. He has come here on the pretext of hunting fish, but his overwhelming presence startles me, captures my attention. Time stops moving here. A god has occupied the river, silent beauty and fear, terror of the beak that comes to you at night to penetrate your eyes and your reason.

A DREAM FROM THE SUBURBS

I'm sorry for the silver strings that are appearing like lightning tentacles in your hair, but it's not my fault. The important thing is what the silver decorates, not its superficial appearance. I like the diamonds and the bracelets that shiver on your sunburnt mediterranean wrists. Time enjoys good company there.

I'm in a deep green forest, with a pipe in my mouth, pondering under the light that seeps through the vault of leaves. There is a turquoise pond where I stick my feet. Yellow waterlilies float by slowly and I drink from the water that tastes like sweet honey.

Then I wake up, hearing the whistle of a nearby early morning train. I look at the dying rose on the table, the remains of beer and wine from yesterday. My life in the suburbs; nothing grows in this place. What am I doing here? I ask the mirror's face.

A WALK IN THE FOREST

I wrote this on an anonymous bench in the forest. I really feel sad for the horses. It is as if we have forgotten them… I really felt guilty.

Returning from campus to the mountain I take a detour through the woods. The rustling of fallen leaves and the sound of the wind in the trees, stir the chilly air around my body.

The sun is shining, reflecting itself on the ice that has formed a hard pattern on the surface. The world of fish, different water organisms and insects have been sealed in silence.

Here I search for solitude on the paths that whirl and twirl, mixing themselves with civilization. The horses seem apathetic, indifferent, as if I were in a dream. The naked trees and the hoofed herbivorous mammals remind me of death. Nature has no intentions, and my existence was sugar-driven insanity. All is forgotten. I will now leave my solitude and return to the world of man.

SEPARATION

My darling sent me home
to roam
along the riverside.
Because I was too lazy to join the army,
the situation became alarming.
Since I wouldn't make the bed
and because I left crumbs of bread
on the tablecloth,
she was unable
to control her emotions.
And I, like a stray wall-bound moth,
clung to her light.
But her eyes widened in fright
of a future cruel.
She armored herself with steel
and a mule's head,
the paint of faith stained the door
that led
to the lower floor.
The roar of engines spread fear
like leaves in the bluish stratosphere.

NOTES FROM THE OAK FOREST

I am Fangorn, I live in the forest. My feet are roots and my face is as ancient as the oaks. I drink from the river and watch how the branches float. The fauns, half men, half goats, treat me well and sometimes I transform into one myself. Today I ran with a deer —great fun— but, as I inspire fear, my presence to them is like that of a hunting spear.

THE WOLVES ARE IN TOWN

The square, dressed in black and white, is overrun by wolves coming from the woods. When winter comes with snowflakes under the streetlights and howling winds that search the streets for empty windows. When the forest and the plains of the countryside are shining like crystal clear imagination. And the plateau of the city is a frozen fact. The wolves are becoming the wild owners of the highlands, they are entering doors and windows, dragging bodies out to freeze. Dreadful screams fill the air and an empty wheelchair tumbles down the stairs. Hollow eyes stare into the cold air in frozen despair and a couple of yellow teeth bite the face with great ease, a frozen face with stone-cold grace.

Sacrifice on the stairs that overlook the pyramid formations. The sight is a reminder of the offerings on the pyramids in the Aztec capital, Tenochtitlan. Bodies tumbling down the frozen stairs. The resistance is filled with anger and boiling blood. Equipped with sparkling red heated coal they roam streets filled with fire. The empty chilling howls of scattered wolves paralyze the members of the crowd, but they are strong and want to reclaim the order of the town. Under a wonderous yellow moon, war is waged upon this plateau. Time crawls in times of war, perhaps spring will come no more.

Today the doctor stepped down. He wears round black glasses and and a waxed mustache. The man is as insane as waves in a cheering crowd, as the lilies and grass that dance and scream at the bottom of the sea. They want to break free, but his mustache is thick and it's not going anywhere.

He comes to inspect the dead, leaving the world of books to collect evidence. Dressed in a cloud of perfume and whiskey, the smell of cigar and the manners of the high bourgeoisie, he is dragging the frozen corpses to the cellar. Muttering about the work of the poor, he drops the dead on the floor. His suit is now hard as frozen curtains, his lungs hardening too. Yet the candle on the wooden table, under the iron tools, is as soothing as the wonderous moon.

As he cuts the smooth thick skin off the face of a landlord, a hairy shining wolf stands at the door. He is looking down, grinning at the doctor. Before the head fell off, he did not understand. Yet the joy of the beast was unmistakeable as he returned out into the raging storm.

SETTING SAIL

Back on the original path, waiting for a spring wind to catch my hair, or a boat to set sail to a foreign land. While cold mist and despair wash away my sins outside the dragon's lair. We set sail now, hoping the blazing winds refuse to ignite our white laughing sails. Follow the seagull afar, which cries out solemnly amid mist on a slippery rock, sleeping on the black surface of jelly-water. The plants of the sea want to grasp us by our feet, but we prevail, eating them in silent contemplation of the clear becoming of a landscape. Oh, but is it not oil in the water? And what is that glowing fly in the sky? What, is it a ball of burning coal or is the breath of the dragon?

IMAGERY

While we celebrate our joys, matters far away, colored by the feelings of today, faded into clouds within our minds, shadows in eternal sunshine, hover above us with hooks of conviction. Rainbow against the red moon, iron curtains or natural thorns? Their roots are the same, but their manifestations are worthy of scorn. Old animals looking for food, on the dusty plains of old, where men play with eyes so cold.

THE ASSASSIN

I bring you snakes from the desert, Sahib.

—Thank you, young Abdul, you may hang them in the closet over there.

—I hang your snakes with the socks, Sahib.

—I am grateful for your services, Abdul; you may leave now.

*The master returns to his studies of the holy scripture.

*A young naked woman with golden writings on her body enters the tent with grace and curves like the dunes of the desert.

—Sahib, I bring you the pleasures of the desert.

*The holy Sahib looks annoyed and says without looking:

—I am grateful for your services, please hang the snakes in the closet.

—Sahib, I am not a snake hunter, I was sent by Sheik Abdullah.

*The hot desert wind fills the air with gleaming sand particles for a moment, the eyes of the woman flash with red hatred. She pulls out a revolver from her right boot, and the holy Sahib rests peacefully over bloodstained parchment.

THE DWARVES

Mist on ice,
frost on the land,
a chilly surprise,
the natural band.
Frost on the ground
and the rise of the morning sun,
I hear winter pound
and summer run.
Ice flakes in the water
shiver and weep,
buried its laughter
as slowly it creeps.
In the dungeon are stalagmites,
like salty teeth,
puffing on their pipes
sit dwarves eating beef.
Singing for black water,
smoking for joy,
the dungeon's daughter,
miserable toy.
Waiting for wind spirits,
they sing and joke,
talk about merits,
lifting their forks.

THE STREAM OF HISTORY

A man was standing on a hill where tall trees pierced the air, casting long shadows around him. Down below was a green forest fair. The man was looking at the river of history streaming by so slow, with statues standing on its shores.

History was running away with the streams and disappeared in a thicker white mist. The woodcutters were designing the slopes around the river, and the flowers came and went with the seasons. The sun was painting the water in relation to the time of the day and silent monkeys fell from dry wooden sticks into the water where they ate fleeting men.

Far away there was an army of monkeys swimming against the stream. When are they going to arrive here? Asked the man on the hill as he silently sat on a stone watching the river. Where am I going to run? I can't go to the future because of the stream, and I cannot go with it because of the monkeys. So, man turned to the heavens where a ladder swiftly fell before his eyes. He walked up with a grin on his face while his eyes turned to the slopes of the mountain, bouncing lightly in the wet evening air.

EVIL WHALES

I dreamed I was a bird that fled from a bear; I flew and flew but the view was dull to the eye and to the mind. They say birds are free, but I felt only despair. I could not descend as there was the bear, awaiting my return. So, I stayed.

The other night I dreamed about passing through the ocean in a big boat watching it through a window. Big fishes were bouncing around. I discussed it with my companions and suddenly, a whale appeared next to the ship. The scene was wonderful, its shining wet skin in the light wild water. But more whales turned up and they started changing the course of the ship with the strength and weight of their dark bodies. In this beauty lay their silent evil. The ship was led to a dead end with high walls surrounding us, preventing all possibilities of escape. High white cement barriers in the night and wild waves thrust against the blocks. The ship sank and we all drowned in the depths of the sea. The whales were nowhere to be seen.

THE BEARDED MAN

At the birth of the day
I leave my nest to hear the birds play,
to let myself bloom
in the present spirit of the sun,
decay was forced to run
as I swung my sword.
Later, that same day,
I was bitter and went to pray,
that no more would I offend
a bearded man with an appearance gray.
The dead of the streets and benches,
who are they,
amidst the dogs and the stenches?
What are they but prey?
Who am I to offend what I do not know
and to judge by the light that glows.
The face is covered with the stench
that society leaves,
yellow teeth of the mouth
through which it breathes.
There is no God, but lies,
lies of a father in the skies,
and the myth of the rise

of his son Jesus Christ.
What can I do but mutter
in this utter world of lilies and lies,
the stench of death
plagues the tormented faces
and embraces
the graveyard with structures of beauty.

THE BEAST WITHIN

Let loose that beast,
let it feast,
let it roam,
let it loose from beneath the tomb,
let it taste that bloody flesh
of innocence.
Let loose the beast from the inner core,
let it loose and don't let it come back evermore.
Let it tear and swear
like a blood-thirsty bear,
let it sit and laugh among dwindling candles
and feast upon the skulls of the victims,
let loose that beast,
if for a moment at least.
It came from underneath,
the sea covered its teeth,
and it crawled ashore
to the world of men.
Screaming with teeth so cold
and a heart so bold,
completely unforetold,
that beast within you,
in your unconscious mind

that is unkind
and harmful.
Let the darkness rule
and slit the head of a mule,
let it be cruel,
take the blood of the innocent
and drink it like wine.
This is what your heart wants,
let it unfold
on a winter's day so cold.
While anxiously you sweat at night,
let loose the fright,
let loose the might
of the beast.

HEAT

The air is hot and damp
in my room,
beneath a crystal lamp,
a golden deer,
a mist of fear,
with snow in my hair
and the roar of a bear,
I swear and I curse
within my lair.
Let me out
on an icy route,
let me roll
on snow so cold.
But who am I to fool,
I am stuck as tobacco in a cigarette rolled,
damp wet flesh
on the chair,
beneath the clothes I wear.
Sweat on my forehead,
a warm bed,
shining lamps,
a hole so damp,
a swamp so hot

with mist and fog.
In the distance a howling dog,
I take shelter behind a rock,
I see fishes swim in the dark water,
I hear wild animals and their slaughter,
I am but a man in the wilderness
far from the calming breeze,
and the ease
of a sandy beach.
Only traffic and cars,
thank God for the bars
and the beer is so cold
that it makes my heart bold.
I let these words unfold
and wish for the return of the cold.
The air feels like wool.
Why am I here, am I a fool?

To the master

Thank you for all your songs
that to your mind alone belong.
You probably had better things to do,
you wrote to those who inspired you to grow.
Maybe you simply had to remain unseen
roaming on pastures green.
I hope you are happy where you are,
driving around in your car,
watching the beauty of a shooting star.
Far away on the other side of the ocean
you set things in motion.
Now just enjoy your life,
your wife
and your gun
if it makes them journalists run.

RAGE

Old men with rings of gold
have sold their soul
to the system,
playing their role,
from the poor they stole
cynically and heartlessly fooled.
While the marginalized lost their goal,
a worker happened to drop a tool
on the head of a fat man with a cigar,
that jumped to a limousine
and killed the ones in the bar.
The falling of a solemn star,
the dreams of men,
the author and his pen.
Is this the society we live in,
is this the kin
that fortune wins
and leaves desperate people
while their golden car wheels spin,
and contaminate the atmosphere.
A worker sheds a tear,
he is ridden by fear,
he has lost his gear

and loses his mind in bottles of beer
while the silly crowds cheer.
Radioactive rain
causes pain,
generation after generation,
and the rich blame it on inflation.
I'm not able to give
because without my money I cannot live.
I sip on a cup of tea,
outside, soon, the temperature
will reach high degrees
and the poor will have to pay their fees,
and the state, their dogs release,
screaming rape and torture,
music silences and the ones with fortune
dance without a thought
on what ought
to be done.

FORTUNE

Flesh so rotten,
bones forgotten
in the graveyard.
You played your cards
the best you could
as anyone would.
At least you gave your mud to the earth,
that is what you're worth,
you dined in high society
and your youth was full of rivalry.
I hope you sleep well.
Who can tell?
To the system as a victim, you fell.
Who could have foretold
that you would get old,
that of no use would be all your gold,
that your precious house would be sold
and into a grave you'd be rolled.
With a worthless cross.
Is it really a loss?
Was it worth the cost?
As in a residence you dwelled
and no one's hand you held,

your lineage and your wealth
could not maintain your health.
In the long run,
as time went by,
inside a silent cry,
a murmuring why.

VICE AND VIRTUE

"I need money", she cried out,
and I need you to stop your vice.
But what is life without a touch of spice?
From the hospital, the sighs,
as from vice an old man dies.
Here I lie and cry and you speak of spice,
the Asian looks distant
while he eats a plate of rice,
the flies fly around a homeless man
who lives with mice,
too much spice makes the salad not so nice.
The gambler pulls up his dice
and the American eats his extra-large french fries.
What is vice and what is virtue?
A bit of decadency won't provoke a curfew.
"What about past lives", says the spiritual,
as she prepares on her altar a little ritual.
Socrates speaks on the square,
made a mess his hair,
yet no one seems to care.
Shut up with your questions and lectures!
They make me feel bad
and enough of them I've had.

Plato writes while armies fight.
Who is wrong and who is right?
Life is full of strife,
the soldier chuckles as he pulls out his knife.
Putin says he's had enough,
puts down his boot and feels so tough.
My will is your law
and you are but a pawn,
fight until you reach their lawns.
They may say what they will,
from my throne I choose to kill,
women and men
with a stroke of my pen.
Can we launch an attack from the west
and deal with the empire?
If so our masters desire?
But this will provoke disaster
and it's not the will of the masters,
as stability is our ability
to fulfill the circle of utility.

THE SOLDIER

"It is good enough"
the man says with a cough.
He shivers from cold
with an arrow in his bowel.
It is good enough for me,
I die now as a tool,
I die a fool, but it's good enough,
he says,
right before a bloodfilled cough.
His eyes turn white
and his mouth fills with foam,
as the white cross awaits him above his tomb.
I was paid well,
I have created space
for my family to grow without outrage,
better not think too much
about good and evil and such.
It gives me headache,
and anyway,
it is all fake.
What do I care?
He mutters to himself,
as a bear takes an arm.

They cannot do any more harm.
His last sigh he breathes.
We did a good deed.
As the earth gets to feed,
life goes on beyond me,
no more fees,
not a single tear,
no more fear.
As he enters a new sphere
the maggots feast on his flesh,
but his spirit breathes air so fresh.
He was just a victim
but it's fine.
Now he lies in the grass
drinking lovely wine
from a red gleaming glass
in the shadow of a big perfume pine.

THE CROW BEHIND THE LEAF

"Stop your rhyme, it's time to work",
said the crow behind a leaf,
with a smile on his beak.
Take some time for books
and think about your looks.
Thank you crow,
if you would just allow,
me to fill this screen,
as if I was in my teens
and had all the time in the world.
"Hahaha", said the bird,
as with his head he leans
towards me with a smirk.
As you please,
but you are not too thin,
you'd better move out on the street,
better move your feet
and leave this sheet,
or your eyes I will beat
and in your place
I will take my seat.
Fine then, my lord,
I will take action.

Just give me some time
because it makes me bored,
after all, it's not a crime,
when from thought to thought you are torn.
Anyway, who are you to say
that dreaming makes me delayed?
Are you afraid,
that my work unpaid
will leave you sad and lonely behind your leaf?
I said to the crow smiling, showing my teeth,
he answered with a chuckle,
I just give advice,
my life is not so full of strife,
do take my words into account,
make some money,
a whole amount,
read your book,
start to cook,
and I will stop by at your window
to have a look,
and the eyes above my beak
will stop taking a peek.